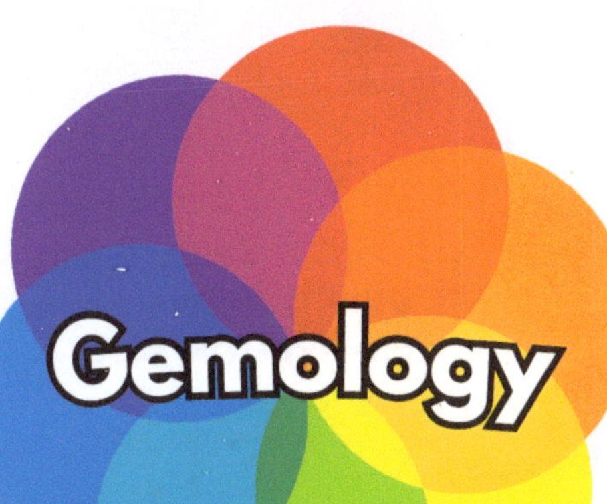

Book of COLORS

A Rainbow of Gemstones

AO PRESS

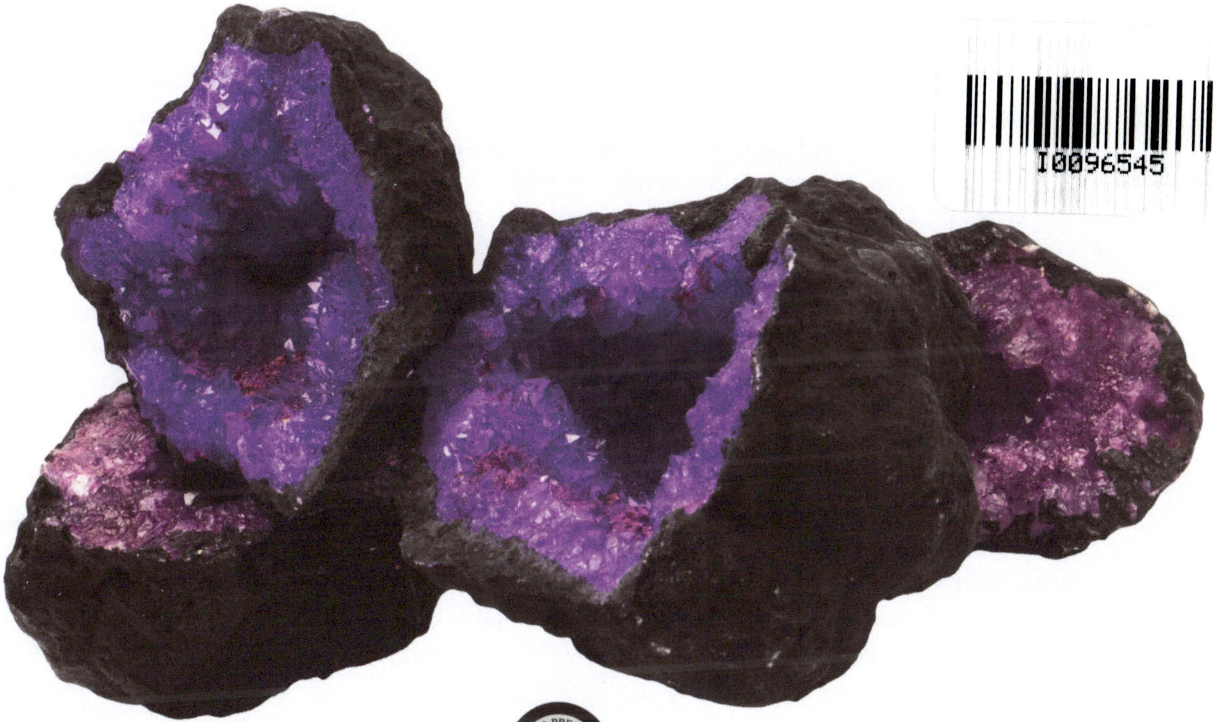

Jessica Lee Anderson

Paperback ISBN: 978-1-964078-23-6

To Chris, Joy, Sam, and Tricia, thanks for sharing your brilliance and encouraging me always! - JLA

Photo credits, left to right, top to bottom: Front cover: Aeya (ruby), lermanikka (citrines), Aeya (emerald), Sunchan (sapphire), Aeya (amethyst), Aeya (pink sapphire); Interior cover: Creative Bird; Copyright page: Aksidesign (emerald cut diamond), avagyanlevon (round cut and emerald cut diamonds); Dedication page: bravo26au; p. 4: KrimKate, vosmanius, vvoevale, Mvorobiev; p. 5: Hariaprionto's Images, Levon Avagyan;, LorenzoT81, Martinan, Vichalian; p. 6: vvoevale, Hans Jaochim, Dan Olsen; p. 7: vvoevale, Peter Hermes Furian, Fred Pinheiro, vvoevale; p. 8: KrimKate, Alexei Jurys, KrimKate; p. 9: KrimKate, avagyanlevon, KrimKate, ValeryVoennyy, p. 10: KrimKate, Aeya, Bogahan, KrimKate; p. 11: KrimKate, Stevenson21, lermannika, KrimKate; p. 12: Kriminskaya Ekaterina, Digiphoto, Aeya; p. 13: Vichalian, KrimKate, vvoevale; p. 14: vvoevale, Ivan Smuk, Aeya; p. 15: jonnysek, ShenderDiana, permian.creations, V&G Studio; p. 16: SunChan, Aeya, Reimphoto; p. 17: Dwlyn Studio, KrimKate, Vichalian, KrimKate; p. 18: vvoevale, KrimKate, vvoevale; p. 19: Stellar-Serbia, KrimKate, vvoevale, KrimKate, Stellar-Serbia; p. 20: vvoevale, real444, onlyfabrizio; p. 21: KrimKate; p. 22: vvoevale, KrimKate, Retouch Man; p. 23: WillScape, KrimKate, burgarstockstar; p. 24: vvoevale, ValeryVoennyy, Vichalian, vvoevale; p. 25: nastya81, Dwlyn Studio, KrimKate, Bureau of Mines USGS, Michel Viard; p. 26: Wirachai Mooncha, vvoevale, avagyanlevon, Nastya22; p. 27: SunChan, Aeya, vvoevale, KrimKate, Hansaki; p. 28: Oksana Tabachenkova, SSpino, SunChan; p. 29: Valery Bazruh, vvoevale, KrimKate; 30: vvoevale, KrimKate; p. 31: rep0rter, Nastya22, Joel Shoemaker, Nastya22; p. 32: beachboy, GummyBone, vvoevale; p. 33: vvoevale, The Stone Sanctuary, KrimKate; p. 34: Michael Anderson; Back cover (agate): Monicore

This Book Belongs to:

____

Gemology is the study of natural and artificial gemstones.

Red black opal

Red

Red aventurine

Ruby

Red sunstone

Gemstones, or gems for short, are also called jewels, precious stones, semi-precious stones, or fine gems.

Rough red carnelian

Red

Garnet

Red sapphire

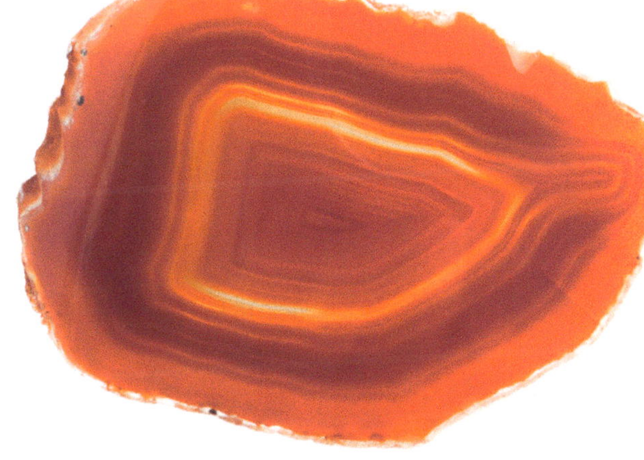

Red agate

Red jasper

Red fluorite

Orange

Orange opal

Amber

Rocks and many kinds of gems are made of minerals, natural substances with crystal structures.

Orange aragonite

Orange

Orange sunstone

Orange calcite

Imperial topaz

Spessartine garnet

Yellow

Yellow calcite

Yellow sapphire

Gems come in a variety of colors! Even the same kinds of gemstones can have variations.

Yellow jasper

Yellow

Rough heliodor

Yellow diamond

Rough citrine

Rough yellow zircon

Green

Green aventurine

Peridot

Tourmaline

Gemologists (people who study precious stones), focus on minerals used as gemstones as well as non-mineral gemstones.

Jade (nephrite)

Green

Rough diopside

Rough beryl

Emeralds

Lace agate

Blue

Gems start out rough, though they can be cut, tumbled, and polished.

Rough blue sapphire

Blue agate

Polished, cut blue sapphire

Blue

Tanzanite

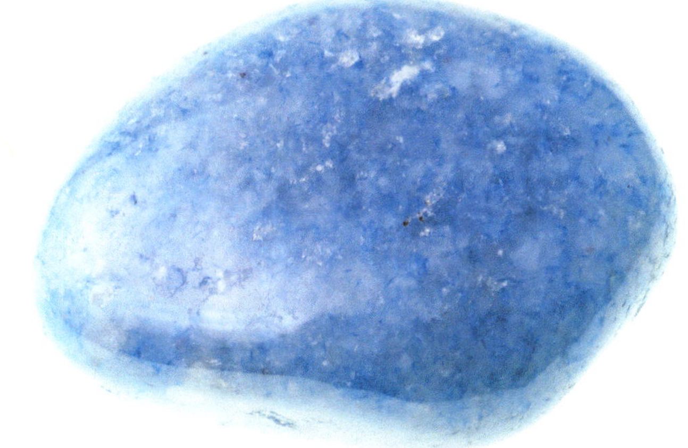

Blue aventurine

Lapiz lazuli (lazurite)

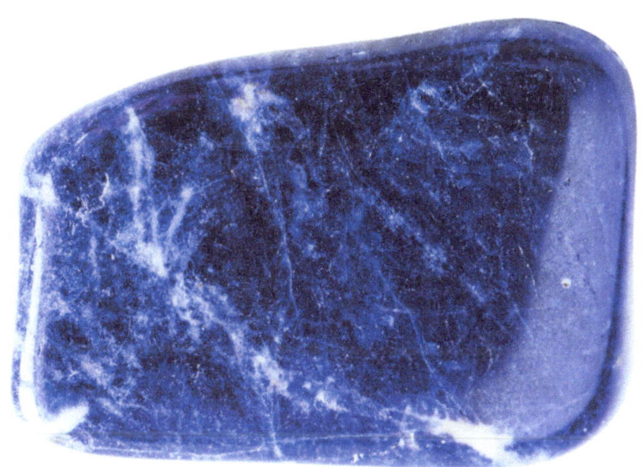

Sodalite

Purple

Stichtite

Amethyst

Gem cutters (lapidaries) create facets—flat, polished cuts to reflect light and enhance the gem's brilliance.

Purple sapphire

Purple

Grape agate

Purple topaz

Fluorite

Kunzite

Pink

Pink tourmaline

Pink diamond

Pink sapphire

Some gems are shaped and polished into a cabochon (or cab for short) that is flat on the bottom and round on the top with no facets.

Pink ruby cabochon

Pink

Rose quartz

Rough rhodolite

Rough morganite

Rough rhodonite

Pink spinel

Black

Rough obsidian

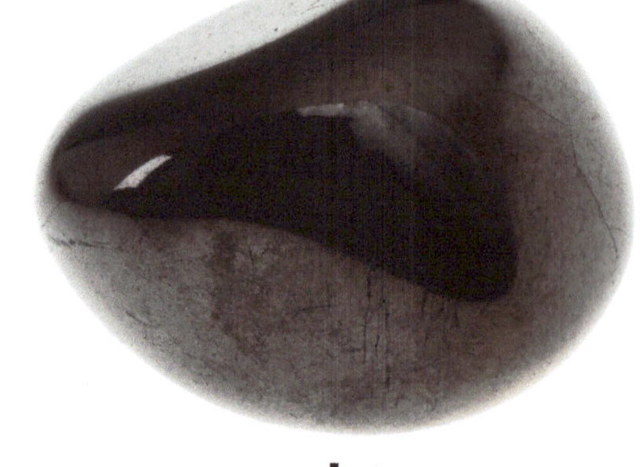

Jet

Hematite

In addition to jewelry, some gems have been used to make ornaments and weapons over the ages.

Diopside

Black

Black tourmaline

Onyx

Rough black anthracite

Rough black spinel

Black amber

White

Moonstone

White calcite

White pearl

Certain gems are iridescent, meaning they give off a brilliant sheen, and some seem to change colors in the light.

Selenite

White
Spodumene
Rough datolite
Rough magnesite
White agate
Quartz

Gray

Hematite

Belomorite

Certain gems are highly prized and often worn by royalty like kings and queens.

Rough diamond

Gray

Smoky quartz

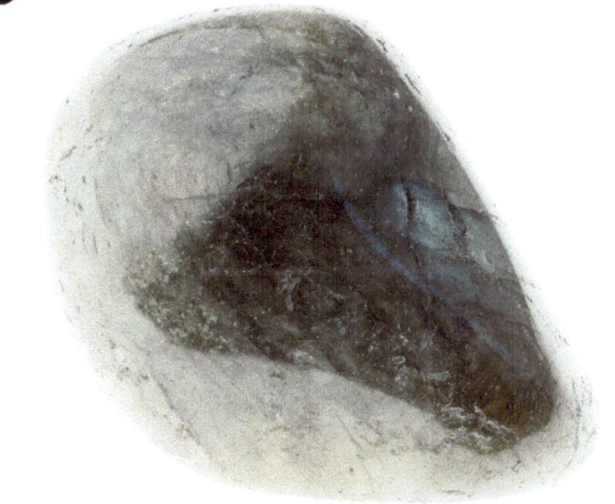
Labradorite

Rough zircon

Chalcedony

Brown

Bronzite

Andalusite

Leopard skin jasper

The value of a gem depends on demand, how rare it is, and the clarity (degree of flaws and impurities).

Hypersthene

Brown

Tiger's eye

Smoky quartz

Obsidian

Brown garnet

Sphalerite

Turquoise

Rough blue topaz

Rough calcite

Turquoise

Turquoise is the only gemstone that has a color named after it.

Celestite

Turquoise

Aquamarine

Alexandrite

Green aventurine

Rough blue apatite

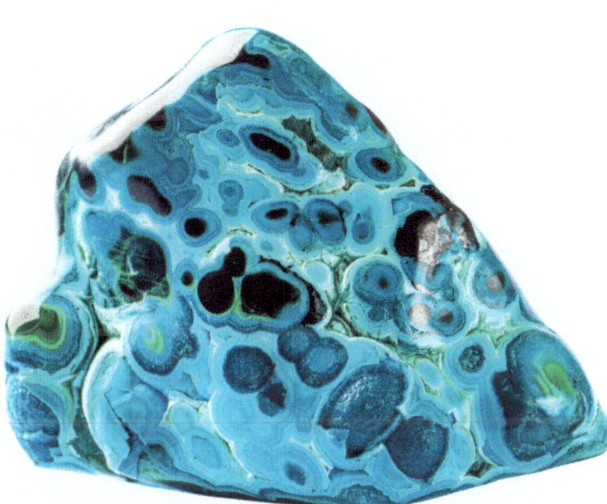

Chrysocolla malachite

COLOR Combinations

Can you describe the colors and patterns of these gems?

Blue opal

Black pearl

Australian opal

Boulder opal

COLOR Combinations

Rough pink beryl

Rough beryl

Rough green beryl

What are some things you notice about the shapes, colors, and features of the beryl samples? Why do you think that matters?

COLOR Combinations

Snowflake obsidian

Zoisite

Pink corundum

What are some colors and features you notice about these gems? Why do you think that is?

Rhodonite

COLOR Combinations

How are these gems similar and different when it comes to colors, shapes, and patterns?

Fluorite

Fluorite

Fluorite

Fluorite

COLOR Combinations

Labradorite

Moissanite

What are some similarities and differences you observe in the colors and features of the gems?

Rainbow pyrite

COLOR Combinations

Jadeite

Bumblebee jasper

Kyanite

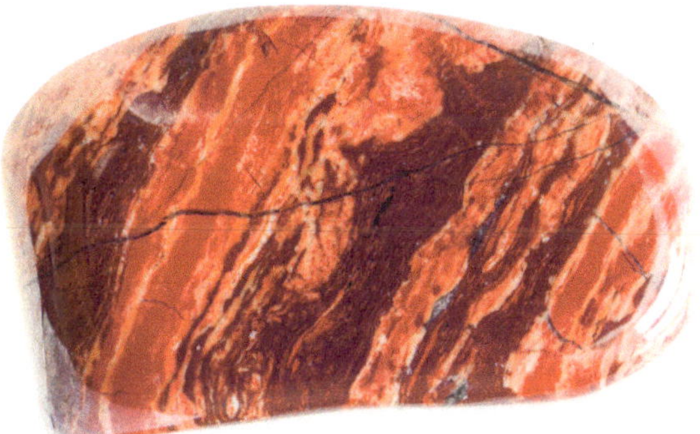
Red jasper

What are the colors, shapes, and physical properties of these gems? How are they the same or different?

Jessica Lee Anderson is an award-winning author of over 75 books for young readers including the NAOMI NASH chapter book series and many reptile books for young readers. Jessica loves spending time in nature and exploring the outdoors with her husband, Michael, and their daughter, Ava! Jessica loves going rock hunting near her home in Austin, Texas. You can learn more about Jessica by visiting www.jessicaleeanderson.com.

Check out these other books:

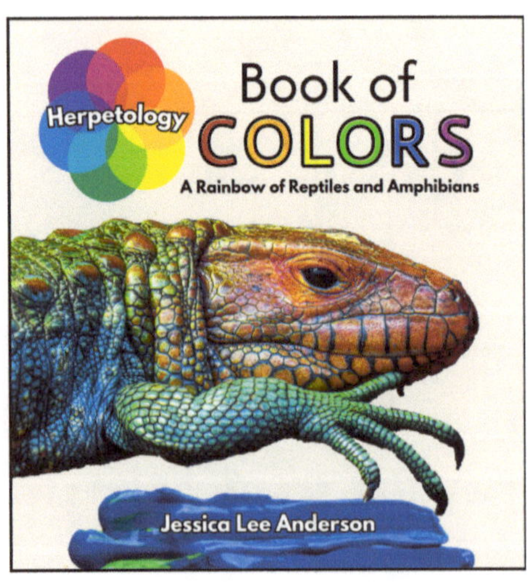

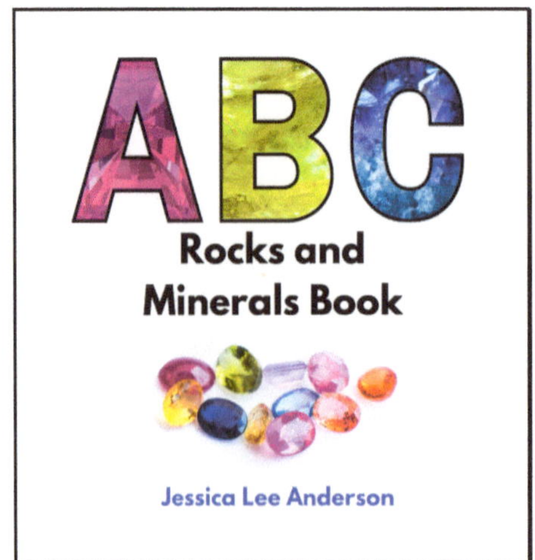

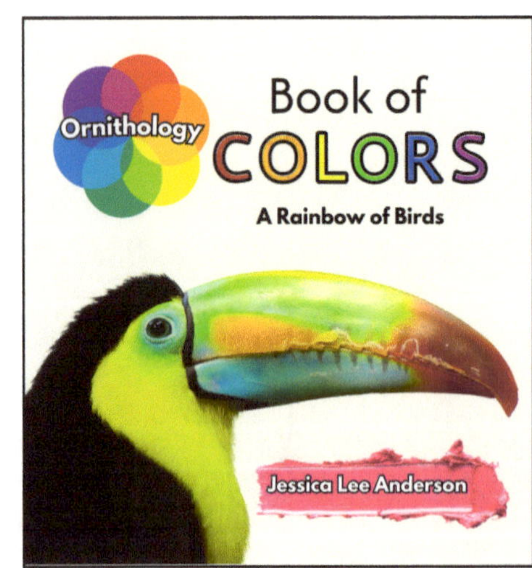

www.ingramcontent.com/pod-product-compliance
Lightning Source LLC
Chambersburg PA
CBHW061144030426
42335CB00002B/99

* 9 7 8 1 9 6 4 0 7 8 2 7 4 *